EDGE BOOKS

Bulldogs, Poodles, Dalmatians, and Other

NON-SPORTING DOGS

by Tammy Gagne

CAPSTONE PRESS
a capstone imprint

Edge Books are published by Capstone Press,
1710 Roe Crest Drive, North Mankato, Minnesota 56003
www.mycapstone.com

Library of Congress Cataloging-in-Publication Data
Names: Gagne, Tammy, author.
Title: Bulldogs, Poodles, Dalmatians, and other non-sporting dogs / by
  Tammy Gagne.
Description: North Mankato, Minnesota : Capstone Press, [2017] | Series: Dog
  encyclopedias | Audience: Ages 9-12. | Audience: Grades 4 to 6. | Includes
  bibliographical references and index. | Description based on print version
  record and CIP data provided by publisher; resource not viewed.
Summary: Informative text and vivid photos introduce readers to various
  non-sporting dog breeds.
Identifiers: LCCN 2015045571 (print) | LCCN 2015043101 (ebook) |
  ISBN 978-1-5157-0299-3 (library binding) | ISBN 978-1-5157-0307-5 (ebook pdf)
Subjects: LCSH: Dog breeds—Juvenile literature. | Dogs—Juvenile literature.
Classification: LCC SF429.B85 (print) | LCC SF429.B85 G3474 2017 (ebook) |
  DDC 636.72—dc23
LC record available at http://lccn.loc.gov/2015045571

Editorial Credits
Alesha Halvorson, editor; Terri Poburka, designer; Kelly Garvin, media researcher;
Katy LaVigne, production specialist

Photo Credits
Corbis/Robert Dowling, 6 (top); Dreamstime: Maigi, 26 (t), Podius, 6 (bottom); Newscom/Dorling Kindersley Universal Images Group, 20 (b); Shutterstock: Andrey Burmakin, 23 (b), AnetaPics, 17 (t), Bildagentur Zoonar GmbH, cover (top right), 15 (t), 18 (t), BORTEL Pavel-Pavelmidi, 13 (t), Capsture Light, 8 (t), dien, 29 (b), Dora Zett, 9 (t), Eric Isselee, backcover, 7 (b), 9 (b), 13 (b), 15 (b), 17 (b), 18 (b), 19 (b), 21 (b), 24 (b), 28 (b), Erik Lam, 26 (b), 27 (b), f8grapher, 7 (t), IMANDRA, 27 (t), Jagodka, 16 (b), Lee319, 22 (t), 24 (t), Lenkadan, 12 (t), Liliya Kulianionak, 12 (b), manfredxy, 28 (t), Mark Herreid, 21 (t), Mitrofanov Alexander, 29 (t), Oleg Znamenskiy, 25 (t), Oliver Tindall, 1, pavelmayorov, 11 (t), Robynrg, cover (left), RTimages, 22 (b), saasemen, 16 (t), Sergey Fatin, 14 (t), Susan Schmitz, 10 (b), steamroller_blues, 25 (b), Svetlana Valoueva, 20 (t), TatyanaPanova, 11 (b), 23 (t), The Dog Photographer, 4-5, VKarlov, cover, (bottom left), 19 (t), WilleeCole Photography, 10 (t)

Printed and bound in the United States of America.
009676F16

Table of Contents

FUN FACT

The AKC is the national dog registry of the United States. The AKC and other kennel clubs around the world divide dogs into groups based on similar traits.

Diverse Dogs

The American Kennel Club's non-sporting group is made up of 20 dog breeds. Dogs in the non-sporting group are all different. These dogs vary in size, coat type, and personality. One breed doesn't even have hair! While each breed is different, they all have one thing in common—they are not used as sporting or working animals.

Some non-sporting group members are wildly popular, such as the Poodle. Others are extremely rare, such as the Tibetan Spaniel. Dalmatians are large, and other dogs are much smaller, such as the Bichon Frise. A couple breeds—the Bulldog and French Bulldog—are known for having wrinkly foreheads. One breed, the Chinese Shar-Pei, has wrinkles all over.

The non-sporting group is the most varied of all seven American Kennel Club (AKC) groups. These fascinating animals come from more than a dozen different nations. Some have been part of the AKC for more than 100 years. Others have been recognized more recently. Get ready for a close look at each breed!

American Eskimo Dog

FUN FACT

The American Eskimo Dog's name is deceiving. The breed was not developed in Alaska or anywhere else in the United States. It descends from the German Spitz.

Appearance:

Toy
Height: 9 to 12 inches (23 to 30 centimeters)
Weight: 6 to 10 pounds (3 to 5 kilograms)

Miniature
Height: 12 to 15 inches (30 to 38 cm)
Weight: 10 to 20 pounds (5 to 9 kg)

Standard
Height: 15 to 19 inches (38 to 48 cm)
Weight: 18 to 35 pounds (8 to 16 kg)

The American Eskimo Dog comes in three sizes: toy, miniature, and standard. All three types have a white, double coat. This hair keeps the dog warm in the winter and cool in the summer. The hair traps cool air in hotter weather.

Personality: American Eskimo Dogs make great family pets, and they are eager to please their human family members.

Breed Background: American Eskimo Dogs were popular circus performers during the early 1900s.

Country of Origin: Germany

Recognized by AKC: 1994

Training Notes: This highly intelligent breed is easy to train, but it is slow to mature. An American Eskimo Dog may behave like a puppy for up to two years.

Care Notes: American Eskimo Dogs need to be brushed and bathed often. These dogs also need about 30 minutes of daily exercise.

Bichon Frise

Appearance:
Height: 9 to 12 inches (23 to 30 cm)
Weight: 10 to 16 pounds (5 to 7 kg)

The Bichon Frise is small but sturdy. It has a curly, double coat and short legs. Because it doesn't shed, the Bichon is a popular pet for people with allergies.

Personality: The Bichon Frise is a devoted and entertaining companion. This lively breed loves attention. Some owners insist that these happy dogs actually smile.

FUN FACT
Many Bichons live between 14 and 16 years, making them one of the healthiest of all dog breeds.

Breed Background: The Bichon Frise is of Mediterranean ancestry and is related to the Maltese.

Area of Origin: Mediterranean

Recognized by AKC: 1972

Training Notes: This intelligent breed can learn tricks quickly. A Bichon Frise can take longer to housetrain than other dogs. Bichons respond well to gentle, positive training.

Care Notes: The Bichon Frise's hair grows quickly. Owners must brush it often and trim it when it gets too long. These dogs have a lot of energy and need daily exercise, including walks.

Boston Terrier

Appearance:
Height: 15 to 17 inches (38 to 43 cm)
Weight: 15 to 25 pounds (7 to 11 kg)

Many Boston terriers have a black and white color pattern that helps them stand out from other dog breeds. But some are seal. This color appears black at first. In certain lighting, it looks red. Others are black brindle and white, brindle and white, or seal brindle and white. Brindle is a **tawny**, streaked color. Boston Terriers are also known for their large eyes and **expressive** faces.

Personality: Boston Terriers are alert, intelligent, and kind. They love people. Boston Terriers are known for their big hearts and clownish ways. They don't bark as much as many other terriers. They do, however, have a few unpleasant habits. The breed is known for grunting, snoring, and passing gas.

Breed Background: The Boston Terrier dates back to 1865. It was created when Bulldogs were crossed with White English Terriers. White English Terriers are now extinct.

Country of Origin: United States

Recognized by AKC: 1893

Training Notes: Boston Terriers are smart but sensitive. An owner's harsh tone can delay training progress. These dogs also tend to be stubborn. Owners should be persistent yet positive whenever working with this breed.

FUN FACT

The Boston Terrier is nicknamed the American Gentleman for its personality and appearance. Some people think this charming dog's dark and white coat pattern looks like a **tuxedo.**

Care Notes: Nearly all dogs love food. But Boston Terriers seem to enjoy eating even more than other dogs. Owners must watch how much they feed their Boston Terriers for this reason. Many members of this breed end up overweight, which can cause health problems. Boston Terriers enjoy daily walks with their human family. An occasional bath and brushing also keep this dog's coat looking its best.

FUN FACT

The Boston Terrier is an American Indian breed.

Bulldog

Appearance:
Height: 12 to 16 inches (30 to 41 cm)
Weight: 40 to 50 pounds (18 to 23 kg)

Bulldogs have large heads, heavy bodies, and short, **bowed** legs. Common Bulldog coat colors are brindle, white, red, or yellow-brown.

Personality: Members of this breed love their human family members deeply. Bulldogs also get along well with new people as long as they are **socialized** when they are young.

Country of Origin: United Kingdom

Recognized by AKC: 1886

Training Notes: Bulldogs can be stubborn and lazy. This breed often needs to be convinced to go for a walk. Because of their stubbornness, Bulldogs can also take longer to housetrain than other dog breeds. Training should begin early and include treats and praise as rewards.

Care Notes: A Bulldog's wrinkles need to be wiped clean with a damp cloth regularly. Even more importantly owners must be extra careful with this breed around water. Unlike most dogs, Bulldogs are not naturally good at swimming.

FUN FACT

Many people call this breed the English Bulldog. Actually, neither the AKC nor the Kennel Club of England use the word "English" in the breed's name. A Bulldog is just a Bulldog.

FAMOUS DOGS

This breed is a symbol of some impressive institutions. A Bulldog is the official **mascot** of Yale University, the University of Georgia, and the U.S. Marine Corps.

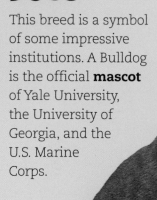

Chinese Shar-Pei

Appearance:

Height: 18 to 25 inches (46 to 64 cm)
Weight: 40 to 55 pounds (18 to 25 kg)

The Chinese Shar-Pei is a unique-looking dog. Covered with wrinkles, a Shar-Pei looks like it has too much skin for its body. The name Shar-Pei actually means "sand skin." The breed's short, rough coat reminds many people of sand.

Personality: The Shar-Pei is a devoted companion and excellent watchdog. The breed can get along with other animals, as long as they are raised together.

FUN FACT

The Chinese Shar-Pei has a blue-black tongue that is most noticeable at the back of its mouth.

Breed Background: These brave animals were developed as palace guards for Chinese royalty.

Country of Origin: China

Recognized by AKC: 1992

Training Notes: Socialization is important for a Shar-Pei because of its stubbornness. The instinct to guard runs deep in these dogs, so they need to be trained at an early age. Chinese Shar-Peis are quick learners.

Care Notes: The Chinese Shar-Pei needs a lot of exercise. Similar to the Bulldog, a Shar-Pei needs its wrinkles cleaned often.

Chow Chow

Appearance:
Height: 17 to 20 inches (43 to 51 cm)
Weight: 45 to 80 pounds (20 to 36 kg)

With its large ruff, the Chow Chow looks like a small lion. Its coat can be rough or smooth and comes in a variety of colors—red, black, blue, cinnamon, and cream.

Personality: Although it looks cuddly, this breed is not known for its friendly nature. Chow Chows take time to bond with people. Once they do, however, they are fiercely loyal. They sometimes can act **aggressively** toward children, strangers, and other pets.

Breed Background: Chinese emperors used this breed for hunting, guarding, and pulling sleds.

Country of Origin: China

Recognized by AKC: 1903

Training Notes: A Chow Chow can be stubborn. For this reason the breed needs early **obedience** training and socialization.

Care Notes: Chow Chows enjoy daily exercise. An inactive Chow Chow is likely to be irritable. They also need regular brushing and bathing.

Coton de Tulear

Appearance:
Height: 8 to 12 inches (20 to 30 cm)
Weight: 8 to 15 pounds (4 to 7 kg)

The Coton du Tulear has a fluffy coat that looks like cotton. The "Coton" part of this breed's name means "cotton" in French. Its hair can be white, black and white, or tricolor.

Personality: Coton du Tulears can live almost anywhere. They make great pets and thrive on human companionship.

Breed Background: Some dog enthusiasts believe pirates brought this breed to the African city of Tulear.

Country of Origin: Madagascar

Recognized by AKC: 2014

Training Notes: These smart dogs learn quickly and love to please their owners. Some members of the breed even compete in **agility**. The Coton is a noisy dog and may bark often, so training should begin right away.

Care Notes: The Coton needs a fair amount of grooming. The fluffy coat tangles easily, so daily brushing is a must. Needing little exercise, this dog is happy with a short walk each day. Some Cotons enjoy swimming.

FUN FACT

The Coton de Tulear is related to the Bichon Frise and the Maltese.

Dalmatian

Appearance:
Height: 19 to 24 inches (48 to 61 cm)
Weight: 45 to 70 pounds (20 to 32 kg)

The Dalmatian is one of the most recognizable breeds in the world. It is known for its spotted coat. Some Dalmatians have only a few spots. Others are covered from head to tail in black markings. Many Dalmatians even have spots on the inside of their mouths.

Personality: Dalmatians can make great pets. They are highly athletic dogs. Dalmatians make great jogging partners for active owners. They also get along well with older children. When happy, these lively dogs are even known to curl their lips into a smile. People who aren't familiar with the expression, however, can mistake it for an aggressive gesture.

Breed Background: Also known as English Coach Dogs, Dalmatians once worked as guards for the horse-drawn carriages of the wealthy. Later they began guarding horse-drawn firetrucks instead. Today the breed is a popular mascot of many fire departments.

Country of Origin: Dalmatia (present-day Croatia)

Recognized by AKC: 1888

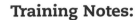

Training Notes:

Dalmatians are smart dogs and easily trained. They cannot be trusted off leash, however. This independent breed is known for its tendency to run away whenever it gets the chance. These dogs often excel in competitive sports, such as agility and rally events.

Care Notes: The short Dalmatian coat doesn't **mat**. It does shed, though. Owners often complain that they find more Dalmatian hair on their furniture than on their dogs. Regular brushing can help remove dead hair. This short-haired breed needs a coat or sweater in colder climates. Dalmatians need a lot of exercise, such as daily running or walking.

FUN FACT

Dalmatians are born without spots. The black markings appear on their white coats as they get older.

Finnish Spitz

Appearance:
Height: 15 to 20 inches (38 to 51 cm)
Weight: 20 to 35 pounds (9 to 16 kg)

The Finnish Spitz looks a bit like a fox. Its square body is covered with a thick double coat. Males usually have fuller coats than females. All dogs are a golden red color and can range from a pale honey to a deep red-brown.

Personality: Developed as hunting dogs, Finnish Spitzes remain highly active. Many Finnish Spitzes still hunt in their native country. They can also make excellent pets for families, because they get along well with kids. Intensely loyal, a Finnish Spitz will protect its human family when necessary.

Country of Origin: Finland

Recognized by AKC: 1988

Training Notes: The Finnish Spitz is a smart dog but bores easily. To keep this breed focused, train often but only for short periods of time. These dogs respond well to positive praise and rewards.

Care Notes: A Finnish Spitz needs a lot of exercise each day. A rigorous play session in a fenced area can help use up this dog's energy. Because it is a heavy shedder, regular brushing and bathing are important.

FUN FACT

The Finnish Spitz is the national dog of Finland.

French Bulldog

Appearance:
Height: up to 12 inches (30 cm)
Weight: 22 to 28 pounds (10 to 13 kg)

French Bulldogs come in several colors. Sometimes called Frenchies, these small dogs may be black, brindle, yellow-brown, or white. They can also be a mix of these colors. Their batlike ears and flat faces add to their distinctive look.

Personality: French Bulldogs make great pets. However their short **muzzles** can get in the way of warm weather fun. Breathing can be difficult for this breed, especially when the weather is hot.

Breed Background: French Bulldogs were created by crossing small Bulldogs with Pugs and Terriers.

Country of Origin: England

Recognized by AKC: 1898

Training Notes: Frenchies strive to please their owners and can be trained easily with positive motivation, such as treats. Socialization with other animals and people should start right away.

Care Notes: Frenchies need their wrinkles cleaned regularly. Grooming their short coats is easy. An occasional bath is all that is needed.

FUN FACT
Contrary to its name, the French Bulldog isn't French. English people brought this breed to France when they moved there from Nottingham.

17

Keeshond

Appearance:
Height: 16 to 18 inches (41 to 46 cm)
Weight: 50 to 65 pounds (23 to 29 kg)

The Keeshond looks a lot like a teddy bear. This breed's double coat is tricolored. Its hair is a mix of black, cream, and gray.

Personality: The Keeshond loves people. Great with kids, this breed makes an excellent family pet. Keeshonden tend to bark a lot, though.

Country of Origin: Netherlands

Recognized by AKC: 1930

Training Notes: Keeshonden enjoy pleasing their owners. They are also smart, so training them is easy. Basic obedience training should begin early on so that good habits are learned right away.

Care Notes: This fluffy breed needs to be groomed twice per week, including brushing. Keeshonden love to explore, so daily walks are recommended.

FUN FACT

Known as the Smiling Dutchman, the Keeshond is the national dog of the Netherlands.

Lhasa Apso

Appearance:
Height: 9 to 11 inches (23 to 28 cm)
Weight: 12 to 18 pounds (5 to 8 kg)

The Lhasa Apso has a long, double coat. Some owners keep their Llasas' hair short to make the hair easier to groom. The coat comes in a variety of colors, including cream, gold, and honey.

Personality: Lhasas are loyal dogs and adore their human family members. Some people describe Llasas as clownish and silly. This small breed can be afraid of strangers, though.

Breed Background: The first Lhasa Apsos in the United States came from the 13th Dalai Lama. He gave the dogs to an American couple visiting Tibet in 1933.

Country of Origin: Tibet

Recognized by AKC: 1935

Training Notes: Llasas can be stubborn, so positive and motivational training is key. Early socialization with other animals and people is important for these dogs too.

Care Notes: Lhasas need a large amount of grooming to keep them looking their best. Weekly brushing is necessary. These dogs also enjoy regular walks.

FUN FACT
The oldest known Lhasa Apso lived to the age of 29!

Löwchen

Appearance:
Height: 12 to 14 inches (30 to 36 cm)
Weight: 9 to 18 pounds (4 to 8 kg)

The Löwchen's distinctive haircut is short on the rump, legs, and tail. Each leg has a fluffy cuff of fur above the foot. The tail has a large **plume** on the end. These dogs come in up to 18 different color variations, including black, black and silver, and chocolate.

Personality: The Löwchen is a gentle, playful breed. It is an affectionate companion to its human family members. Löwchen can be a bit shy with strangers. They warm up quickly to other animals, though.

Country of Origin: Germany

Recognized by AKC: 1996

Training Notes: Löwchen bark a lot and will alert their owners to whatever might be going on nearby. They can make good watchdogs for this reason. Owners must train these dogs so they don't bark excessively.

Care Notes: The Löwchen coat doesn't require a great deal of care. Some brushing is necessary to keep the hair from matting. Because of its high energy level, the Löwchen enjoys daily exercise, including walks.

Norwegian Lundehund

Appearance:

Height: 12 to 15 inches (30 to 38 cm)
Weight: 13 to 16 pounds (6 to 7 kg)

This small dog has a short, double coat. Some Norwegian Lundehunds have red-brown hair that is black on the tips. Other members of this breed are black or gray with white markings. Some are white with black or gray markings.

Personality: This curious breed can make a good pet with proper training and supervision. Lundehunds tend to bark and dig a lot.

Country of Origin: Norway

Recognized by AKC: 2011

Training Notes: This breed is known for being difficult to housetrain. Sticking to a strict schedule is important for Lundehunds. Early socialization is also helpful for these sensitive dogs.

Care Notes: Because of their short coat, Norwegian Lundehunds only need an occasional bath and brushing. However, their fast-growing nails should be trimmed regularly. These active dogs love to go for walks or play in a fenced area.

FUN FACT

The Norwegian Lundehund has six toes on each foot. Most dogs have only four per foot.

Poodle

Appearance:

Miniature
Height: **11 to 15 inches (28 to 38 cm)**
Weight: 15 to 17 pounds (7 to 8 kg)

Standard
Height: **over 15 inches (38 cm)**
Weight: 45 to 70 pounds (20 to 32 kg)

The Poodle comes in three different sizes. The smallest Poodles are members of the toy group. Miniature Poodles and Standard Poodles are members of the non-sporting group.

These curly canines come in many colors. Black, brown, and white dogs are the most common. Poodles kept in one of the breed's traditional haircuts are easy to spot. Their coats include large puffs of hair as well as shaved areas. Many pet Poodle owners trim their dogs' coats more evenly.

Personality: Poodles are popular pets—and for good reason. These smart, lively dogs are a lot of fun to have around. Poodles are incredibly loyal and loving. Protective of their owners, they often make great guard dogs.

Breed Background: The word *Poodle* comes from a German word meaning "puddle." This is fitting because the breed began as a hunting dog in northern Europe. Poodles are excellent swimmers and would retrieve game from water.

FUN FACT

Some Poodles have been crossed with other breeds to make other allergy-friendly breeds. A Cockapoo was created by crossing a Poodle with the Cocker Spaniel. A Labradoodle is part Poodle and part Labrador Retriever.

Country of Origin: Germany

Recognized by AKC: 1887

Training Notes: Poodles are regularly ranked among the most intelligent dog breeds. Despite this fact they still need training to make pleasant pets. The biggest mistake a Poodle owner can make is thinking that these dogs naturally know how to behave properly. A bored Poodle can get into a lot of trouble!

Care Notes: This breed's hair doesn't shed like many other breeds. For this reason Poodles are a great choice for people who are allergic to the **dander** found on many other dogs. Owners who want to keep their Poodles looking like show dogs must be prepared to groom their pets a lot. Some owners rely on a professional groomer for this important task. This breed's fast-growing coat can make these appointments frequent and expensive.

The Poodle is an active breed that needs daily exercise. It excels at hunting and agility events.

FUN FACT

Over time the Poodle's hair will cord naturally if it isn't trimmed. The cords look like dreadlocks.

Schipperke

Appearance:
Height: 10 to 13 inches (25 to 33 cm)
Weight: 12 to 18 pounds (5 to 8 kg)

The Schipperke is a small, black dog with pointed ears. The short, double coat is longer behind the dog's ears and around its neck.

Personality: This breed is known for its mischievous ways. A Schipperke seems to have no idea how little it is. These tiny dogs are also known for maturing slowly. Some are four or five years old before they start acting like adults.

Country of Origin: Belgium

Recognized by AKC: 1904

Training Notes: Training is especially important for this stubborn breed. If an owner doesn't take the lead, the Schipperke surely will. The Schipperke is smart, though, so training isn't difficult.

Care Notes: This active breed needs plenty of exercise. It does best when it has a fenced yard so it can run around and play often. Although Schipperkes shed, they usually only require weekly brushing.

Shiba Inu

Appearance:

Height: 13 to 17 inches (33 to 43 cm)
Weight: 17 to 23 pounds (8 to 10 kg)

The Shiba Inu's pointed ears and reddish coloring make the breed look like a small fox. This breed has a short yet thick coat. The dense fur actually repels dirt, making the Shiba Inu one of the cleanest dog breeds.

FUN FACT

The Shiba Inu is one of the most popular pet dogs in Japan.

Personality: The Shiba Inu is loyal and loving. Because the breed is independent, some people see the breed as unfriendly. Many owners compare the Shiba Inu's personality to that of a cat. They love their owners—on their own terms.

Breed Background: This ancient breed was developed to hunt birds, bears, and boar.

Country of Origin: Japan

Recognized by AKC: 1992

Training Notes: This breed is known for being one of the toughest dogs to train. Early puppy socialization and obedience classes are needed for these strong-willed dogs.

Care Notes: Another reason people liken Shiba Inu to cats is that these dogs are fussy about their appearance. They constantly self-groom. Owners still have to brush these dogs to keep shedding to a minimum.

Tibetan Spaniel

FUN FACT

Tibbies like to **perch** at the highest spot in the room. Being up high gives them the best view of everything going on within the household.

Appearance:

Height: 10 to 11 inches (25 to 28 cm)
Weight: 9 to 15 pounds (4 to 7 kg)

The Tibetan Spaniel is a small dog that looks like a little lion. The breed's silky, double coat is smooth on the animal's face and the front of its legs. The hair is longer on the rest of the animal's body. Similar to a lion, a mane of long hair covers this dog's neck. The coat can be any color or mix of colors. Tibbies have plumed tails that curl over their backs. Feathery hair also grows from between this dog's toes.

Personality: Tibetan Spaniel lovers prefer these dogs for many reasons. One of the biggest reasons is how affectionate these animals are with people. Tibbies are sensitive to their owners' feelings. When people are sad or upset, this breed is right there to comfort them.

Tibetan Spaniels make wonderful family pets. They love being included in activities and thrive when owners give them plenty of attention. This friendly breed loves older kids.

Country of Origin: Tibet

Recognized by AKC: 1983

Training Notes: Tibbies can be stubborn at times, but they learn easily. To help this breed become a reliable pet, owners should begin training when the dog is a puppy.

Care Notes: The Tibetan Spaniel's coat is easy to groom. A walk or two each day is enough to fulfill its exercise needs. These curious little dogs must be kept on leashes in public because of their natural curiosity.

FUN FACT

Tibbies get along with other dogs, and even cats, extremely well. This easygoing breed does well in multi-pet households.

Tibetan Terrier

FUN FACT

The Tibetan Terrier's nickname is the Holy Dog.

Appearance:

Height: 14 to 16 inches (36 to 41 cm)
Weight: 20 to 24 pounds (9 to 11 kg)

The Tibetan Terrier has long, fine hair that may be straight or wavy. The double coat comes in a variety of colors and combinations. White, gold, and silver are among the most popular.

Personality: This adaptive breed enjoys spending time indoors and out. While they don't need lots of exercise, they are more than happy to join in any activity. They just want to spend time with their favorite human family members—wherever that may be.

Breed Background: This breed was developed by Tibetan monks called lamas.

Country of Origin: Tibet

Recognized by AKC: 1973

Training Notes: The Tibetan Terrier is easy to train. However, this dog gets bored easily. Owners who use plenty of praise and food rewards usually see the best results.

Care Notes: Tibetan Terriers need a large amount of grooming. As they grow into adults, their coats also grow. A dog needs daily brushing during this period to prevent tangles. A fully grown Tibetan Terrier needs to be brushed about three times per week.

Xoloitzcuintli

Appearance:

Height: **18 to 23 inches (46 to 58 cm)**
Weight: 25 to 40 pounds (11 to 18 kg)

If it weren't for its unusual name, the Xoloitzcuintli (*show-low-itz-KWEENT-lee*) would stand out from other breeds mostly for its looks. Also known as the Mexican Hairless, this breed isn't completely hairless. It does have a small amount of hair on its back, tail, and the top of its head.

Personality: Called the Xolo for short, this breed can make a great pet. These dogs get along well with kids but prefer older children who know how to behave around them.

Breed Background: The Xoloitzcuintli is one of the oldest dog breeds in the world. Because this breed is naturally warm, ancient Aztec people slept with the Xoloitzcuintli close by to stay warm.

Country of Origin: Mexico

Recognized by AKC: 2010

Training Notes: The Xolo needs consistent training and lots of praise. Regular socialization with other animals should be maintained throughout its life.

Care Notes: Unlike other breeds, the Xolo doesn't require brushing. Instead, its owners must care for its skin. This breed is prone to acne and other skin conditions. Keeping its skin clean and moisturized helps prevent these problems.

FUN FACT

About one in every five Xolo puppies is born with a full coat of short hair.

FAMOUS DOGS

The Xoloitzcuintli breed appears in many paintings by Frida Kahlo and Diego Rivera.

Glossary

aggressive (uh-GREH-siv)—strong and forceful

agility (uh-GI-luh-tee)—the ability to move fast and easily

bow (BOH)—to bend in an outward curvature

dander (DAN-duhr)—skin flakes in an animal's fur or hair

expressive (ek-SPRESS-iv)—filled with meaning or feeling

mascot (MASS-kot)—a person or animal that represents a sports team or organization

mat (MAT)—a thick, tangled mass of hair

muzzle (MUHZ-uhl)—an animal's nose, mouth, and jaws

obedience (oh-BEE-dee-uhns)—obeying rules and commands

perch (PURCH)—to sit or stand on the edge of something, often high up

plume (PLOOM)—a long, fluffy feather often used as an ornament on clothing

socialize (SOH-shuh-lize)—to train to get along with people and other dogs

tawny (TAW-nee)—a brown-orange to light-brown color

tuxedo (tuhk-SEE-doh)—a suit for men to be worn on special occasions

Read More

Furstinger, Nancy. *Dogs*. The Smartest Animals. Minneapolis, Minn.: Core Library, 2014.

Guillain, Charlotte. *Dogs*. Animal Abilities. Chicago: Raintree, 2013.

Steele-Saccio, Eva. *Dogs*. Look and Learn. Washington, D.C.: National Geographic Society, 2014.

Internet Sites

FactHound offers a safe, fun way to find Internet sites related to this book. All of the sites on FactHound have been researched by our staff.

Here's all you do:

Visit *www.facthound.com*

Type in this code: 9781515702993

Check out projects, games and lots more at
www.capstonekids.com

Index